The Way Forward

A HANDBOOK FOR A-LEVEL, SCOTTISH HIGHER GRADE AND IB STUDENTS

Robert Crossan

Robert Crossan is an A-level teacher with twenty years teaching experience.

We wish to thank all the students and staff who have helped in the research and preparation of this book.

Editor: Maura Juffkins
Design: Mouse in the House
Print: Heanor Gate Printing Ltd

Further copies may be obtained from:

Pearson Publishing, Chesterton Mill,
French's Road, Cambridge CB4 3NP

Tel: 0223 350555
Fax: 0223 356484

ISBN: 1 85749 002 9
Price: £4.95

Published 1991 by Pearson Publishing

© Pearson Publishing

No part of this publication may be copied or reproduced, stored in a retrieval system or transmitted in any form or by any means electronic, mechanical, photocopy, recording or otherwise without the prior permission of the publisher.

Contents

		Page
1	Introduction	1
2	Further study?	2
3	Which subjects?	6
4	Course planning	8
5	Time planning	9
6	Settling in	11
7	Classes	12
8	Teachers	13
9	Working together	14
10	Note-taking	15
11	Private study	18
12	Reading skills	19
13	Essay writing	21
14	Practical work	23
15	Coursework	24
16	Fieldwork	26
17	Self-assessment	27
18	Relationships	28
19	First year exams	31
20	Holidays	33
21	The second year	34
22	Mock exams	35
23	Revision	37
24	Examinations	38
25	Illness	42
26	Higher education	43
27	Other options	46
28	Scotland	48

29	Grants and loans	49
30	Job hunting	52
31	Interviews	55
32	A year off?	57
33	Exam results	61
34	Retakes	63
35	Self-employment	65
36	Useful books	67

Appendices

A	Syllabus and coursework chart	70
B	Two year planner	72
C	Weekly timetable	74
D	Important dates to remember	75

1
Introduction

The Way Forward: A-Level is a handbook designed to accompany students at all stages of A-level, Scottish Higher or IB examinations and encourages personal, as well as academic, development.

Consideration is given to adjusting to the higher level of study, establishing and maintaining good working practices, extra-curricular activities, revision and exam technique and career planning. Useful books and addresses are noted throughout the publication and at Chapter 36, page 67.

Many students and teachers have contributed by reviewing draft versions of the text and offering feedback. We have incorporated their comments wherever possible. The handbook also includes quotes from the students.

Outline timetables etc are included in the appendices and these can be adapted for your own use.

We would appreciate any comments you have on the handbook as we are planning to update it regularly.

2
Further study?

You may have already decided which course and subjects you wish to pursue. However, if you are still unsure the following chapter may help you. We have only devoted a few pages to this, as there are many other sources which are available to you. Some of the relevant texts are referred to in this chapter and at Chapter 36, page 67.

The decisions that you make now are important. Remember that decision-making is a long process and not an event. Don't worry too much if it takes you some time to decide your next step.

Many students opt for A-levels as their course of action after GCSEs, or 'Highers' after Standard Grade in Scotland; however, it may be that a vocational, skills-based course, such as BTEC, would suit you better. You may find that *It's Your Choice* published by COIC (Careers and Occupational Information Centre) offers a useful insight into the options that are open to you. It is available from COIC, Moorfoot, Sheffield S1 4QP Tel: 0742 594568. If you want information on BTEC then contact BTEC, Central House, Upper Woburn Place, London WC1H 0HH.

The following is background information on A-levels, Scottish 'Highers' and International Baccalaureate.

A- and AS-levels

A-levels cover a wide range of subjects, and most A-level students complete their course in each of three subjects over a two year period. AS-levels were introduced in 1987 to broaden A-level study. They are the same standard as A-levels, but have a reduced syllabus and take half the teaching time of an A-level. Two AS-levels count as one A-level. You may wish to combine A- and AS-level courses (eg two A-levels and two AS-levels). *Your Choice of A-levels*, published by Hobsons Publishing (see page 68), offers advice on choosing A-level subjects.

Scottish 'Highers'

The counterpart in Scotland of the GCSE is the standard grade of the Scottish Certificate of Education (SCE). Once students have sat the Standard or Ordinary (which is currently being phased out) Grade examinations, they can proceed to the Higher Grade of the SCE.

'Highers', as they are known in Scotland, are taken a year earlier than A-levels and it is common for students to take up to five Higher Grade subjects.

In addition, there is a Certificate of Sixth Year Studies (CSYS) which may be taken by a student who is normally in the sixth year of secondary schooling (ie over 18 years) and who already possesses a pass grade at Higher Grade in the subject concerned. Up to three subjects may be taken in any one year. CSYS is not normally required but it is often recognised as a university entrance qualification.

Information on Scottish examinations may be obtained from the Director, Scottish Examination Board, Ironmills Road, Dalkeith, Midlothian EH22 1LE Tel: 031 663 6601. (See also Chapter 28, page 48.)

International Baccalaureate

'I am really enjoying the course - there is a lot of work but the added range of interesting subjects makes it worth the effort.'

Tom

The International Baccalaureate (IB) Programme is a two-year pre-university course. It is designed to promote international understanding and provide students with a balanced education.

There are currently about 23 institutions in the UK offering this course at the moment. IB replaces the GCSE and A-level exams thus allowing students from abroad, without GCSEs, to study in this country. It is becoming increasingly popular with students as the wide subject base means that students can keep doors open for as long as possible. It also allows access to universities throughout the world. IB does, however, require greater effort as, some people suggest, it is equivalent to about 4.5 A-levels.

For information on IB contact the International Baccalaureate Office, Pascal Close, St Mellons, Cardiff, South Wales CF3 0YP Tel: 0222 770770.

If you think you would like to continue to study, examine why you feel this is appropriate for you. For example, it could be because:

▲ your friends are planning to continue their studies

▲ you can't think of anything better to do

▲ you would like to go on to higher education

▲ you really enjoy a particular subject

▲ it seems to be a natural progression

▲ jobs that attract you are difficult to find.

Having thought about it, are the reasons which you have both logical and practical? Or would it be worth seeking further advice?

Points to bear in mind are:

▲ your choices after GCSE may determine what careers or courses you can pursue in the future

▲ everyone develops at a different speed and some students are better suited to sixth form study and flourish at that stage or vice versa

▲ starting a course is no guarantee of academic success

▲ a pass grade D or E can still open many doors to higher education or jobs

▲ A-level courses require commitment and aptitude.

3
Which subjects?

At this stage, if you feel that you don't know all the options open to you and are not sure if you are making the right decision, then talk to your teachers and careers advisors for information and advice.

If you are undecided on your career, it's a good idea to choose those subjects which interest you and which you are good at. However, you should ask yourself not only *'Where does this lead me?'* but also *'What will this course of action prevent me doing in the future?'*. You may well change your mind halfway through your course, so try to keep your options open for as long as possible.

If you think that you will want to go on to further study after leaving school, ensure you know what subjects are required for which higher education courses. You may be surprised to learn, for example, that not all universities require you to have taken biology A-level or Higher in order to do medicine. It you want to opt for AS-levels, check which higher educational institutions accept combinations of A- and AS-levels.

The following points may help you decide which subjects to choose:

▲ Does the subject interest you? – generally one of the best reasons for choosing a subject.

▲ Studying linked subjects eg maths and physics has obvious benefits.

▲ I like the teacher – this may well be a short term reason as teachers often leave for new jobs, maternity leave etc.

▲ The department has a good success rate in examination results – this is reassuring and may be a good reason for choosing a third subject.

▲ I obtained good results at GCSE – this indicates an ability in the subjects but is not necessarily a good predictor of future results.

▲ My friends are doing them – this is not a good reason on its own.

Before you finally decide which subjects or course you will take, read the syllabus for each subject carefully. (Ask your teachers which exam board you would be following, and where to contact them if they cannot provide the requisite information.) You may find that it is not what you expected. Some subjects have syllabus choices, for example, history. If you have doubts, discuss them with your teacher. Although there will inevitably be parts of any course you will not enjoy, at least make an informed choice before you begin. If your decisions are well thought out, there will be a greater likelihood that you will enjoy your course.

Once you have chosen your subjects, you may wish to make a note of the exam board and syllabus details in the table at Appendix A (page 70). (In Scotland there is only one exam board, see page 3.)

4
Course planning

Planning your course in advance can save you time and anxiety, especially in your final year. On the planning chart (see Appendix B, page 72), make as detailed a timetable as you can at the start of your course. Many dates will be set for you by your school/college or the examination boards. These will include the times of internal mock examinations, field courses, work experience, and the final examinations themselves. You may well, however, have some flexibility over coursework.

Many A-, AS-level, and Higher syllabuses will require you to produce coursework as well as sit examinations. Coursework may be short essays, each counting for a small percentage of your total mark, or a major project or investigation counting for as many as half of your marks. The examination board will set a final date by which your coursework has to be completed. It is likely, however, that your teacher will ask you to hand it in well before this date.

It is vital that you find out how much coursework you will be doing and when it will need to be handed in.

Enter this information on your two year chart. You can then anticipate potential clashes over important work and may be able to negotiate in advance with your teachers over completion times.

Your course will probably be made up of six terms. The actual coverage of the syllabus will not be evenly divided as, for example, the first will probably start slowly, the third will lose out to internal exams and summer activities and the final term will be lost to revision and the exams.

In other words, first year exams are more than half-way through the course and fifth term mocks may cover more than 80% of the syllabus.

5
Time planning

'You don't have to lock yourself away to achieve good grades, just be consistent in getting the work done.'

Andrew

Once you have established the outlines of your course, you can start to plan your week. You will find it an advantage to devise a timetable. In reality timetables can easily be ignored as the pressures of work escalate, but it is useful to develop a routine of work.

If you are taking three A-levels or five Highers you will generally need to spend up to 35 hours a week on your academic work (including lesson time) to complete the assignments you have been set. You will also need to find time to relax and you may also decide to fit in a part-time job. The example in Appendix C (page 74) may help you to work out a schedule.

Much of this advice is obvious but it will make life easier for you if you actively consider all you have to fit in. Be realistic about what you can achieve. For example, you may find that single free periods are best used to relax with friends so that you are able to concentrate your mind more fully in the next lesson.

Remember also that you may not always know when an extra piece of work will be set. It is therefore important to build a degree of flexibility into your schedule. Organising your academic work and not leaving everything until the last minute will help.

You may be forced to make some difficult decisions about part-time work. Many students work on Saturdays and celebrate their freedom on Saturday night. This makes a waking-up time of 7am on Sunday somewhat problematic! If you work in a supermarket, bar or restaurant, you may be offered evening work as well. Consider this carefully. If you are spending more time on paid part-time work than extra study for your courses, you are in danger of not doing enough academic work.

A timetable for your first term

When you know your fixed activities, lessons, sport and other regular events, make yourself a 7-day timetable from say 8am to 11pm each day.

Enter fixed activities, your favourite TV programmes and any part-time work. Then you will see how much time you have for academic work. If you find difficulty in maintaining this schedule, be prepared to reconsider your priorities and draw up a new planner.

As commitments change, it may be worth drawing up a new timetable at the beginning of each term.

6
Settling in

'In retrospect I did enjoy doing A-levels. I found them interesting, but there is a waste of time in your first term making the transition.'

Simon

The change from GCSE to A-level or work can be alarming and it may take you some time to adapt to it. This is usual and you should not worry unduly. You will find that you are much more on your own. Self-discipline and self-motivation will be needed.

A new school or college

'Why has everyone else read so much more than me?'

Carole

You may feel as Carole did but it is worth remembering that you will be one of many settling in and it is likely that others will feel the same. Moving to a new school or college will offer you exciting new opportunities, but will require acclimatisation to more than just a new level of study.

Returning to education

If you have been absent from formal education for a while you may feel a lack of confidence. Do not worry, as you will probably find that you slip back into it quicker than you think. Your advantage is added maturity and almost certainly greater commitment to the courses you are taking.

7
Classes

'Ask a lot of questions. Make the most of your teachers and lecturers.'
Hilary

Much of the information and practice you will need for your examinations will be given in class. It would be useful to try to find out from your teachers what the topics will be for each lesson and read ahead so that you are not meeting totally new material every lesson.

Lessons given to small groups should allow discussion and easy questioning. Do your best to participate and remember that asking questions is not necessarily a declaration of ignorance.

Lectures to larger audiences give teachers more time to prepare handouts and audiovisual materials. They may also be supplemented by tutorials for very small groups. Mark in your notes or on any handouts the points that you do not understand. Make sure that you refer back to these problems and seek out the lecturer to ask any necessary questions.

8
Teachers

'A-level is a lot of hard work but it can be made easier by using the teaching staff to the full – they've seen it all before.'

Neema

It is primarily the teacher's responsibility to make sure that the syllabus for each subject is covered. This will be done through lessons, reading which you are given to do, and the written work which will help you to use your knowledge. If the amount of work that your teachers set seems unreasonable, discuss it with them.

You may find that you do not see eye-to-eye with all teaching staff. It is useful to bear the following in mind:

▲ both you and your teachers have the same aim

▲ even the best teachers cannot think or work for you

▲ teachers you find dull may well achieve good results

▲ teachers actually derive personal as well as professional satisfaction from the success of their pupils.

If you are still unhappy after you have talked through your problems with your teacher, there are steps you can take. You can arrange to see the head of department or faculty. You should have a personal tutor or a director of sixth form studies who can also give advice.

Many teachers are disappointed by how seldom students ask for help. They do not mind being bothered.

9
Working together

'The second year sixth formers helped me a lot. Next year I am really worried that the first years will be asking me questions!'

Nick

Friends can help you a great deal during your course. They can often solve problems which you may be finding difficult but do not wish to discuss with your teachers. Talking through work with others tests whether you have really understood the material yourself. However, ultimately you will be assessed on your own understanding, not that of your friends, so if you have persistent problems, see your teachers.

10
Note-taking

'I never know what to note – I write everything down in case it is important.'
Jason

In lessons

Successful note-taking is often the key to success. It may be possible for your teacher to give you outline notes as a handout at the beginning of each lesson. However, it is more likely that you will have to take your own notes. If the teacher is going too fast for you to take notes, say so. If an unfamiliar word is used make sure you find out what it means.

The value of notes lies in the use you can make of them, not as evidence that you were present at the lesson. Therefore:

▲ try to assimilate the information as it is being said

▲ your notes must be legible – don't write more words than necessary

▲ use abbreviations, create your own as long as you are sure that you will know what they mean later!

▲ use clear headings

▲ learn to recognise what is essential – your notes should be a summary of the lesson

▲ read your notes regularly.

Ideally, you should go over your notes as soon as you can after the lesson, while it is still fresh in your mind, and fill in any gaps. However, this is often not possible and so your notes should be understandable without having to re-write them. Make your notes as clear and visual as possible by using headings, sub-headings, underlining, different colours and illustrations or figures where appropriate. The main points should be easily recognisable. Leave some space on the page for adding extra notes at a later date.

If you have to miss a lesson make sure you go through a fellow student's notes and make your own from them.

Note-taking from books

Making notes independently from a number of sources is something every A-level or Higher student has to do. The difficulties are in deciding how much to note, the style in which to record it, how to use the information, and where to store it so that it can be found again.

▲ How much to read?

Do you need to read the whole book, or are some sections more relevant than others? Using the contents page and index can save you time in the end.

▲ How much to write?

The reason why you are making notes will affect the style, and quantity of them. Are you reading for information, or for comment and interpretation?

If you are reading for information you may well need to make very detailed notes from one or two books. Your teachers should be able to tell you which are the most reliable books from which to do this. Reading for comment and interpretation can lead to much shorter notes. Try to avoid copying out great chunks of text – it is a much better test of your understanding to summarise in your own words the argument of the author. Direct quotations should be brief and the source noted.

▲ What style?
Your notes are for your use, and it is best to develop a style which suits you. You may prefer continuous writing, short points, or some form of flowchart. The essential thing is that they are clear to you.

There are some basic rules to follow:

▲ always note the author, title, publisher, and date of publication
▲ if you are quoting directly from the book, note the page number
▲ start a new piece of paper for each book you consult as this makes filing easier.

Filing

'I was forced to refile all my notes after I dropped them in the bank.'

Mark

You could soon gather enormous files of material. The danger is that without devising a filing system, these files become unwieldy and unusable.

The important things are:

▲ to have a file for each subject
▲ to use dividers to section the work into separate topics
▲ to file essays with the notes – this will make revision easier
▲ you may wish to carry with you only the notes you require in lessons – this will help avoid the dangers of losing or damaging all your notes.

11
Private study

'To succeed you have to be dedicated and really want good results. I don't believe that it is possible to swan through A-levels. Otherwise you are just wasting everyone's time.'

Alison

Everyone will develop his or her own patterns of private study but the following may help you:

▲ getting started is the difficult part

▲ good organisation is most important

▲ set realistic goals

▲ never believe your friends when they talk about the amount of work they are doing!

12
Reading skills

'Read different books to get an alternative view on the same subject.'
Nick

Most subjects will require you to do some extra research. If you are studying English or History you will have a great deal of reading to get through. You will probably have reading lists with some advice on those texts which are most useful to buy. Often, students who have just completed their course have books which they will be willing to sell at a reduced price. Some sixth-forms organise this in a formal way. If you have to buy new books, then forming a syndicate with trustworthy friends to buy a different book each can be a way of increasing the number of books in circulation.

If you are studying a foreign language, then exposure to as much authentic material as possible will be of benefit. You may be able to subscribe to a magazine. Ask your teachers to suggest which ones they think would be most useful.

Make the most of your school and public libraries. Public libraries take most of the major newspapers and journals eg *The Times, Independent, Guardian, Financial Times, Daily Telegraph, Economist, Spectator, New Statesman and Society*. These will keep you up-to-date with current happenings, something which may well be a requirement in subjects such as economics, law, science etc. Remember that you will get marks in exams for points on current affairs and topical issues. You may also find that there are TV programmes or films that are relevant to your course.

Reading skills

When reading, try to understand the material and think critically as you read. Consider whether:

▲ it is fact, opinion or fiction

▲ you are convinced by the arguments

▲ you have learnt anything from the material

▲ it relates to your existing knowledge.

Try to read from different sources so that you get a balanced view of the subject.

Adopt the most suitable reading style. For example:

▲ To extract the main ideas, skim read, paying particular attention to section headings, main words, summaries and conclusions.

▲ To extract detailed information, skim read to get an overall feeling for the text. Then read the material again, making a note of major points. Read it for a third time, making detailed notes under headings.

▲ To learn more about a familiar subject, avoid note-taking. Just read and understand.

You can increase your reading speed by using a bookmark which will allow your eyes to read a sentence at a time rather than just one word. Try to ensure that your eyes do not flash back over words and sentences you have read but maintain smooth progress forwards over the text. There are other specific techniques for speed reading. If you are particularly interested in this then your teacher or careers adviser may be able to help you. Management and Skills Training (MaST) is an organisation which runs courses on effective reading techniques and speed reading. They can be contacted at the MaST Organisation Ltd, Hermitage House, Bath Road, Taplow, Maidenhead, Berks SL6 0AR Tel: 0628 784062.

13
Essay writing

'Do not leave the reading, the research and the writing to the last minute – that way you easily get behind.'

Paul

Essay writing is an art. Some people find it easier than others but everyone should aim to improve their style.

Extended essays may be something new to you and you may have to write thousands of words to a title of only one sentence. The style of writing will be different with the essays requiring more detailed analysis and interpretation. Developing an analytical essay style needs practice and time.

Give yourself enough time to do the subject justice. Plan the content in advance and think about your approach. This will allow you to express yourself as well as you are able.

The following tips may help:

▲ Read the title carefully and make quite sure that you know what it means.

▲ Do the necessary research, which may involve more than just reading your textbook. Your teacher should give you a relevant booklist.

▲ Try to think up an original approach.

▲ Make a plan, with main and sub-headings.

- ▲ Write the essay in rough, taking care over grammar, spelling and paragraphing.
- ▲ Read it through with a critical eye to ensure you are answering the question.
- ▲ Make any alterations to improve what you have written.
- ▲ Write it out legibly.

All of your essay writing is practise for exams. In an exam you will probably only have 35-40 minutes per essay. The examiner will be impressed by:

- ▲ ability to present knowledge in a coherent way
- ▲ good spelling and use of language
- ▲ logical, well-reasoned argument with examples to illustrate points
- ▲ a clear, labelled diagram, if appropriate
- ▲ relevance of the answer to the question
- ▲ depth of knowledge ie have you read around the subject?

You may prefer to type your essays but remember that you will not be able to type in the examinations, so do not lose the skill of writing quickly and legibly.

Wordprocessing

Some courses may require you to type or wordprocess essays, especially if they are for coursework. Wordprocessing enables you to write and revise easily, especially useful if you change your mind! If you have had no experience of wordprocessing, try to persuade your school or college to provide courses for you – almost certainly there will be the necessary machines in the building.

14
Practical work

'My main problem is writing up practicals in time.'

Tim

Practicals are an essential part of A-level courses in science and technology. Many A-levels have a practical examination as part of the final assessment, while several syllabuses have practicals spread over the two years as part of their continuous assessment programme.

Remember:

▲ Prepare for your practical by checking your knowledge of the theory behind it.

▲ Read the instructions carefully.

▲ If you usually do practicals with a partner, make sure that you gain experience of using all the equipment. There is no substitute for doing something yourself.

▲ Record your results as accurately as you can.

▲ Complete your writing up while the experience of the practical is still fresh.

▲ Just as much can be learned from an experiment that fails as from one that succeeds.

▲ Try to sort out problems for yourself if you can.

Art, music and drama courses will also have practicals to which some of the above points will apply.

15
Coursework

> 'Think carefully about opting for subjects with coursework elements – there are a lot of benefits, but it also puts an immense strain on your work during the two years and your subjects could suffer.'
>
> Louise

Many subjects require you to produce coursework which can count for as much as 50% of your marks. Coursework can be a series of short pieces, usually set by your teacher, or a major investigation which you have to choose for yourself.

It is essential that you know how much coursework will be expected from you, when this is going to be due, and how it will be marked.

Coursework requires planning, concentration and sufficient time for research and writing so that your other work is not adversely affected.

The following tips may help:

▲ Often you will not have a choice but if you do, choose a subject that interests you.

▲ Start preparing early as things can, and will, go wrong.

▲ Read as widely around the subject as you can.

▲ For a science subject, devise and carry out experiments meticulously. Always write up the method used. Add graphs and tables if relevant.

▲ Write up project work soon after completing it but allow yourself time for reflection to ensure you have covered all the relevant points.

▲ Seek assistance from teaching staff whenever necessary.

▲ Safety is important and it is worthwhile mentioning any precautions that you have taken.

▲ Add a bibliography, and any other sources.

> *'I know many people who were too busy with coursework to begin revision.'*
> Janet

You may be tempted to give coursework priority over all other work because it counts towards your final grade. This can lead to a neglect of non-coursework subjects until as late as the revision period in the second year. By then it will be too late. If you have problems fitting in coursework assignments and normal work, signal this early in discussion with your course adviser and work out a plan to give a proper balance between your subjects.

16
Fieldwork

'Taking into consideration that I studied languages, I should have gone to both France and Germany during the two years.'

Carl

Fieldwork can range from a day course to three weeks in a foreign country. Residential field courses are normal in subjects such as biology and geography. Coursework is often based upon them, while examination questions may well require you to give examples from such coursework. In addition, other departments may arrange extended visits eg Art History in Paris. Such courses can be very worthwhile and indeed are often the highlight of the course as you explore your subject and grow closer to your teachers and fellow students. You need to discover:

▲ Whether a field course is compulsory.

▲ What are you likely to learn on them? How much work will be done on the course and what commitment will there be afterwards?

▲ Whether you are expected to pay for it. If so, how much? Is there supplementary funding available through the school or education authority?

▲ What work in other subjects you will miss if you go on a field course in term time.

17
Self-assessment

'Always keep your goal in mind as an incentive.'
                                                    Angela

Your school or college will have a formal system to review your progress, but it will be to your benefit to assess yourself more frequently, at least once a term.

A simple analysis might look at:

▲ Your strengths and weaknesses, likes and dislikes.

▲ Whether you are facing the same problems in more than one subject.

▲ If your problems are getting better or worse.

▲ What is helping to solve or aggravate any problem.

▲ Where are the best sources of help?

Consider also:

▲ Whether your work is of the required standard. Your teacher's marks will tell you this. Do not let matters slide if you are consistently achieving low marks.

▲ Do you need to change your way of writing, reading or note-taking?

▲ Do you need extra help from your teacher? If so, what?

18
Relationships

Parents

'My mum's on her own, so I have to spend a lot of time with her.'

Kate

' I wish my parents would get off my back!'

Brian

Studying for A-levels or Highers can be seen as a sacrifice. You are giving up the possibility of immediate earnings to gain qualifications to assist you in the future. It is also a sacrifice for your parents as you will probably be living at home, which means that they will be providing you with food, warmth and somewhere to stay. Parents are sometimes expected to buy books or to pay for field trips, although it is possible that you will be contributing by earning your own money through part-time work.

Problems will no doubt arise through your wish to be independent and your parents' concern for your well-being. Consider the situation from their point of view and ask yourself whether you would prefer your parents to nag you or to be totally indifferent towards you. Do you take them into your confidence or leave them ignorant of things that may be bothering you? There are no easy answers and everyone will experience difficulties to varying degrees.

It is worth remembering that your parents are probably finding it difficult to adapt to your growing independence.

If you have problems of any kind you can contact NAYPCAS (National Association of Young People's Counselling and Advisory Services) at 17-23 Albion Street, Leicester LE1 6GD Tel: 0533 554775.

Friends

'I could have worked harder, but only at the expense of my social life, which was an unacceptable sacrifice.'

Karen

Karen decided that her social life was too important to sacrifice. Your social life will increasingly revolve around your friends rather than your family. Among friends you can develop your own personality and interests. However, you may have to face some difficult and uncomfortable decisions.

Drink

'We go to the pub every Friday. It's something to do.'

Sam

You will be very much aware of the laws on drinking. Bear these in mind and also consider what you would do, given that you are one of a crowd:

▲ Will you refuse to travel with a driver who is drinking?

▲ How will you get home?

▲ How strong is your sense of self-preservation?

Drugs

'I hate people who drop drugs into your drinks at parties.'

Ann

There may be other pressures as well. What would you say if you were offered illegal drugs by a friend? Say 'No'? End the friendship? Inform the police? Take the drug? Remember AIDS. Can you stop? If you cannot, but want to, and need to talk to someone you could contact your local Citizens' Advice Bureau who will be able to advise you in confidence of any self-help groups in the area, or whether the local health authority has their own counselling service and Drug Dependency Unit.

You can also contact SCODA (Standing Conference on Drug Abuse) for information at 1-4 Hatton Place, London EC1N 8ND Tel: 071 430 2341. If you have problems relating to drugs and the law contact RELEASE who have a 24-hour helpline Tel: 071 603 8654.

Love

'My boyfriend ditched me at the start of the exams and I couldn't work properly because I felt so wretched.'

Jane

No one can predict when he or she will fall in love, how intense the relationship will be, or how long it will last. You may be fortunate and find a partner who compliments your personality, and provides great emotional stability and support. This is particularly true if your partner understands your ambitions and the pressures of being a student.

The Family Planning Association provides free and confidential contraceptive advice and contraceptives. You can find your local branch by looking in the phone book or by contacting the headquarters of the Family Planning Association at 27-35 Mortimer Street, London W1N 7RJ Tel: 071 636 7866. Condoms, as you probably know, can be bought in any chemist shop, most large supermarkets and some pub toilets. Avoiding pregnancy is the responsibility of both partners. If you do become pregnant, or your girlfriend does, proper advice should be sought immediately, either through her family doctor or organisations such as the Brook Advisory Centres (see below) or the British Pregnancy Advisory Service.

There are Brook Advisory Centres throughout the country. They provide a free service where young and unmarried people can go for advice and practical help with birth control, pregnancy, sexual and emotional problems.

In London, contact them at 153a East Street, London SE17 2SD Tel: 071 708 1390. Your local Brook Advisory Centre will be listed in the Yellow Pages.

19
First year exams

'First year exams were the biggest shock I had during A-level.'
Ben

Ben was obviously completely unprepared for his first year exams. It is important therefore to do yourself justice by preparing for them; they are an important test of your organisation and understanding. Coming more than half-way through your A-level course, they are often used as the basis for important decisions about your future, such as whether or not you will continue with all your subjects.

UCCA/PCAS applications require schools to give estimated grades for each subject a candidate is taking. Many teachers use the results in the first year exams as a basis for their estimated grades.

It is therefore essential that you allow enough time to prepare for these examinations because:

▲ It is unlikely that your teachers will devote any lesson time to revision. They will be too busy trying to move through the syllabus.

▲ You may have other pressures on your time such as coursework to produce or work-experience to be done.

▲ You are unlikely to have sat examinations of this type before.

▲ You will have far more material to absorb than for GCSE.

By Easter of the first year you should be:

▲ re-reading your notes

▲ making précis of essential facts or formulae

▲ learning material

▲ looking at past papers to acquaint yourself with the style of questions and to practise preparing essay plans.

If you do this, you have a better chance of showing something of your true ability in the first year exams. Treat them as an opportunity to practise your revision and examination skills.

After the first year exams you will normally have a full review of your performance so far, and will have to draw up plans for the second year. If you are advised to do some academic work over the summer holiday, do so, because time will pass so quickly that you will have no chance to catch up.

If your performance in the first year exams was not as good as you hoped then discuss with your teachers how they feel you can improve. You may feel that you do not want to continue with the course. This should not necessarily be regarded as a failure but as a chance to change course to something which would suit you better.

20 Holidays

'I did all my coursework in the holidays. I had no time during the terms.'
Peter

Holidays are used for resting, having a complete change and possibly for earning some money.

Holidays can also be used for catching-up on work for your course. As term time will inevitably be reduced by illness, examinations, field courses, interviews etc, holidays are the most likely time you will have to consolidate your work, check your notes are complete and understandable, and to catch up on any work left undone during the term.

Research for projects or coursework can also be tackled and languages can be improved by travelling. You will almost certainly have to use Easter of the second year for revision.

In summary, try to plan to use your holidays constructively but ensure that you leave some time to relax and enjoy yourself.

21
The second year

'You may have to cut back on some of your extra activities.'
David

You will by now have a good idea about how you are doing. Take time to think about how you will fit in your study and how best to aim for the exams ahead. It is a good time to redo your timetable and to reassess your commitments. Also give serious thought to what you want to do next. Students often feel very uncertain about their future at this time. So don't feel that you are abnormal if you do!

It may be that you have decided you do not want to proceed to higher education now, but would prefer to start work . However, do not make any rash decisions as, even if you did not fare well in the first year exams, there is still time to knuckle down to hard work if you really want to.

22
Mock exams

'They showed me the areas where I was weakest and where I needed to improve.'

Nick

There is never a perfect time for mock exams in the second year. You may have them before Christmas or sometime between January and March. At whatever time they are set, you are likely to have covered over 75% of the course.

The first year exams will have given you an indication of what to expect, but there will be a lot more pressure on you now. Mocks will be the nearest approximation to the real A-levels that you will have and there will probably be little or no class time devoted to revision.

So, in preparation for your mocks:

▲ What lessons did you learn from the first year exams which you can apply to your mocks?

▲ Are your notes in a state from which you can revise?

▲ Have you left enough time for some realistic revision? Many students hate having to work over Christmas and New Year, but this may be the only time you have.

After your mocks, you will be given results and debriefs by your teachers on your performance. This will help you in the technical aspects of answering the questions set.

More important are the lessons you learn for yourself. Consider:

▲ Was the result a fair reflection of your ability at this stage?

▲ What areas of the syllabus did you find most difficult? How can you improve?

▲ What style of revision worked best for you? What did not work?

If you did do well, remember that mocks can breed a false sense of security. Bear in mind that:

▲ you will not have covered the whole syllabus yet

▲ your teachers will have chosen a paper that you are likely to be able to do to give you confidence in your ability

▲ the examiners will always try to devise a new angle for each exam.

23 Revision

'Learn as you go along, so that it isn't a rush at the end of the course when you realise that you don't actually know anything!'

Richard

You will probably face mock exams in the fourth or fifth term, and the real thing at the end of the second year. Do not leave your revision until it is too late. Allow plenty of time for a gradual and sustained revision plan.

▲ Devise a realistic revision timetable which incorporates work for all the sets of exams.

▲ It is likely that your concentration time will last effectively for 30 to 40 minutes – you may therefore need regular short breaks.

▲ Try not to revise more than two subjects on one day.

▲ If you've come to the bottom of a page and can't remember anything, have a break!

▲ Practise doing past exam questions under exam conditions.

▲ Use your essays and notes to make revision notes to revise from but don't spend all your time making notes – you have to learn them!

▲ Aim to have skeleton revision notes to scan at the last minute.

24
Examinations

'It's useful to write brief notes in case you lose your train of thought.'
Una

Some of the following points are obvious but people have been known to forget under pressure. Therefore:

Before

▲ Know where and when each exam will take place.

▲ Have your exam slip or timetable handy.

▲ Collect all you will need: pens, pencils, rubber, rulers, calculator, tissues, watch, spectacles (if you need them).

▲ If you suffer from an ailment (eg hay fever or painful periods), remember to take the appropriate medication in advance.

▲ Leave home early enough to arrive on time.

▲ Listen carefully to the invigilator's instructions.

▲ Fill in the front of your exam paper carefully.

Exam technique

▲ If you get nervous take a few deep breaths to try and calm yourself.

▲ Be sure about the number of questions you must answer, and if there are any compulsory ones.

- ▲ Read through the entire paper before starting your answers and to look at both sides of each sheet.
- ▲ Give yourself a positive start by doing the questions you can answer best.
- ▲ Start each question on a clean sheet of paper.
- ▲ If you're writing essays, divide your time sensibly and evenly and don't think you're saving time by not writing small essay plans.
- ▲ For each question spend about five minutes planning your answer. A well-constructed, concise answer will earn you more marks.
- ▲ If there are calculations, show the workings.
- ▲ Allow enough time to read through and check your answers.
- ▲ Remember: no answer means no marks. It's better to write a sketchy outline than nothing at all.
- ▲ The first 50% of marks of a question are usually much easier to get than the remaining 50% in most subjects, so ensure that you attempt the full number of questions stated.
- ▲ Do not speak or hand anything to anyone while in the examination hall, even at the end of an exam.

Oral exams

Orals can be more nerve-racking than written exams because you are 'performing' in front of the examiner. You should have rehearsed a number of possible situations such as conversations about your family and what you do in your free time. However, you must not give the impression that you are repeating what you have learned by rote.

On the day of the oral exam:

- ▲ speak slowly, loudly and clearly, with expression

- listen very closely to the questions and comments
- make sure what you say is relevant
- eye contact with the examiner is important and will help you to concentrate
- you should only use your hands to emphasize what you are saying – try not to fiddle
- remember – you can steer the conversation to topics you prefer
- even if you are spoken to in the *tu* form in French or the *du* form in German, you should reply in the *vous* or *Sie* form
- ask the examiner to repeat the question if you do not understand it.

Practical exams

Many of the points on exam technique also apply to practical exams. However, the following are extra points to be aware of:

- follow all safety rules and make a note of precautions in your write-up
- make sure the equipment and materials are available for when you need them
- set a target for what you are going to do in each session (if there is more than one)
- plan your schedule so that you do not waste time waiting for something to dry or cool
- use aprons, face guards, gloves and fume cupboards when necessary
- label your work with your name, candidate number etc as instructed.

Exam problems

You will probably experience a great deal of stress and anxiety at exam time. This is normal. You must, however, try to control your feelings and relax.

If you suffer from hay fever, painful periods or some other medical problem, seek advice from your doctor. Remember also that some painkillers can cause drowsiness. (See the following chapter on Illness.)

25
Illness

'I had a very interrupted second year because of glandular fever.'
                                                                Mary

'I was not at my best during the examinations because of hay fever.'
                                                                Ged

Ill-health affects some students during their course or examinations. This can include acute menstrual problems. Take advice as early as you can, particularly if you are likely to be prescribed the pill. Examination boards and universities will take medical problems into account if you follow the usual procedure:

▲ Obtain a certificate from your doctor straight away, indicating what your illness was and for what period you were unable to work properly.

▲ Make some photocopies of this. The school/college may do this for you. Keep a few copies for yourself.

▲ Take the certificate to your examinations officer. This teacher will consult your normal teachers, obtain the grades they predicted for you and send these with your medical certificate to the Examination Board.

▲ Write at once to your first- and second-choice universities enclosing a copy of the medical certificate. This may be important in helping them decide what to do if you narrowly fail to gain the grades they require. It is best to notify them as soon as possible.

26 Higher education

Before filling in any forms there are key questions to ask yourself.

What are your needs?

- ▲ Is higher education right for you?
- ▲ What kinds of courses might be open to you?
- ▲ Do you enjoy studying?
- ▲ How does higher education fit in with your career intentions?
- ▲ Would any degree subject enable you to do what you want to?
- ▲ Which courses would interest you?
- ▲ How can you keep as many doors open for as long as possible?
- ▲ What decision timetable do you have?
- ▲ How likely are you to achieve the grades required to do the course you want to?

Which course?

- ▲ What is the content of the course?
- ▲ What options are there within the course?
- ▲ Is it full-time or part-time?
- ▲ Do you have to travel abroad or work on an industrial placement?
- ▲ What grades are required?

Where are you going?

▲ How far from home is it?

▲ What kind of accommodation is available?

▲ What are the surroundings like?

▲ Do you have any special needs – for example proximity to white water canoeing may be as valid as the course content!

Entry to higher education is usually at 18 years or older. Once you have considered all of the questions above you will be better placed to consider a higher education course. Such courses lead to degrees, diplomas of higher education (DipHE), HND or similar awards.

You may wish to read *Higher Education and You* published by Wiltshire Guidance Services and available from The County Careers Centre, Bythesea Road, Trowbridge BA14 8EZ. (Contact them for price details.) The publication gives an overview of the choices available to you and has a useful section on higher education and Europe.

ECCTIS (Educational Counselling and Credit Transfer Information Service) is a national computerised service giving details of further and higher education courses with entry requirements and other information. It is available from careers officers and is on Prestel and TAPs (Training Access Points). Contact ECCTIS at Fulton House, Jessop Avenue, Cheltenham, Glos GL50 3SH Tel: 0242 518724 or your careers office.

As you will discover, there is an amazing range of different courses to choose from.

Making applications

Applications to many sectors of higher education are made through central 'Clearing Houses'. Clearing Houses enable applicants to apply on one form for a number of different courses. They make it easier for higher education institutions to match available places to students. UCCA and PCAS are the two major Clearing Houses. UCCA stands for Universities Central Council on Admissions; PCAS is the Polytechnics Central Admissions System. For 1992 entry onwards there is a joint application form as UCCA and PCAS systems have combined, so you can apply for university and polytechnic courses at the same time.

The UCCA handbook can be obtained free of charge from: UCCA, PO Box 28, Cheltenham GL50 3SA Tel: 0242 222444. The PCAS handbook can be obtained free of charge from PCAS, PO Box 67, Cheltenham GL50 3SF Tel: 0242 526225. The same application form covers admission to a first degree, DipHE or HND course, through UCCA or PCAS. When you ask for the application form, you will be sent the handbooks which will guide you as to how to fill in the form.

Check the handbooks carefully because colleges and institutes of higher education also usually insist on application through the central system. Applications for teacher training are now handled by the Clearing Houses at Cheltenham. The Central Register and Clearing House (CRCH) booklet gives details of all initial teacher training courses (ie normally BEd degree) within the CRCH scheme. It is available free of charge from the Central Register and Clearing House, 3 Crawford Place, London WlH 2BN.

If you intend to take a year off after A-levels you can ask for deferred entry. If you do, higher education establishments may need to be convinced that you'll use your year out constructively; so be prepared to tell them what you plan to do (see Chapter 32 A year off? p 57).

27
Other options

There are a number of courses for which you should make a direct application, without going through the UCCA/PCAS scheme. Some of these are detailed in this chapter.

Art and design courses
The majority of non-university art and design degree and Higher Diploma applications are handled by the Art and Design Admissions Registry, Penn House, 9 Broad Street, Hereford, HR4 9AP Tel: 0432 266653.

Colleges of music
The major colleges or schools of music run courses that can be divided into graduate level courses and those leading to licentiate or associate qualifications. There are also courses described as diplomas or certificates which are regarded as equivalent to a degree for grant purposes.

You should contact the institution to find out the entry qualifications. Some schools require a minimum of two A-levels and a high standard of music proficiency for graduate courses, and the same level of musical proficiency but lower academic qualifications for non-graduate courses.

For further information, look at *Careers in Music – Just The Job* published by the Music Advisers National Association, available at careers centres; *Careers in the Music Business* published by Kogan Page and *British Music Education Yearbook* published by Rhinegold Publishers Ltd.

Secretarial colleges

The three principal examining boards are The Royal Society of Arts Examination Board (RSA); The Pitman Examination Institute (PEI); and The London Chamber of Commerce and Industry (LCCI).

Most private secretarial colleges are centres for these boards and although there is no formal accreditation body the great majority offer a high standard of instruction.

Additionally a number of the more widely-known secretarial colleges are members of the Independent Secretarial Association (ISTA).

Private colleges are listed in Yellow Pages and your careers adviser should be able to recommend a good one in the area.

The Independent Schools Careers Service (ISCO) publishes a *Directory of Independent Further Education Colleges* which lists the secretarial colleges. Contact ISCO at 12a-18a Princess Way, Camberley, Surrey GU15 3SP Tel: 0276 21188.

28
Scotland

This chapter contains brief details regarding further and higher education possibilities for Scottish students in Scotland. General information is detailed on pages 43 to 47.

Students interested in a vocational course should contact the Scottish Vocational Education Council (SCOTVEC), 38 Queen Street, Glasgow G1 3DY. SCOTVEC makes awards for a wide range of courses in the technical and business sectors.

Scottish students intending to go to Scottish universities must apply after Standard Grade. The full-time first degree course in Scotland is generally four years for an Honours degree and three years for the broad-based Ordinary degree. *The Scottish Universities Entrance Guide* published annually by the Scottish Universities Council on Entrance, 12 The Links, St Andrews, Fife KY16 9JB is a useful source of information.

Entry to English institutions of higher education is also possible on the basis of Highers ie 5 Highers ≈ 3 A-levels; 4 Highers ≈ 2 A-levels.

COIC (Careers and Occupational Information Centre) produce many useful careers publications. Contact them for a copy of their brochure at COIC, 5 Kirk Loan, Corstophine, Edinburgh EH12 7HD Tel: 031 334 0353.

29
Grants and loans

'Most importantly, apply for your grant as soon as you get the form!'

Una

Financial support for students comes from two sources (excluding sponsorship and parents) ie grants and loans, which together form a single system. The information given here is very general and you will have to find out how the regulations affect you personally. For example, do you qualify for a mandatory award or will you have to go through a selection process (eg audition for drama college) before being considered for a discretionary award? (Note that mandatory means the local education authority [LEA] must pay and discretionary means that it is not obliged to pay.)

An award is the money paid by your LEA towards your living costs (ie grant) and your tuition (ie fees). The fees element of your award is normally paid, in full, directly to your higher education establishment by your LEA.

Grants

Grants are means-tested and there are standard scales for estimating how much you are entitled to. If, for example, your family has a taxable income of up to £10,000, you are likely to get the full grant, which is currently £2,265 (£2,845 in London). If you do not receive a full grant, a parental contribution is also calculated on income. The law does not however, compel parents to pay. If they don't do this, you are in for a hard time, as it is difficult enough to make do on the full grant. Students in England and Wales should write to their LEAs for information about grants.

Student Grants and Loans: a brief guide is a leaflet available from the Department of Education and Science, Publications Despatch Centre, Honeypot Lane, Canons Park, Stanmore, Middlesex HA7 1AZ Answerphone: 081 952 2366 or your LEA.

Scottish students should send their application for a student's allowance to the Scottish Education Department, Awards Branch, Gyleview House, 3 Redheughs Rigg, South Gyle, Edinburgh EH12 9HH Tel: 031 244 5869. Your application should be accompanied by a document from the university/college making an unconditional offer of a place. *Student Grants in Scotland – A Guide to Undergraduate Allowances* is available free from the above address.

Students in Northern Ireland should write to their local Education and Library Board. *Grants and Loans to Students* is available free from the Department of Education, Scholarships Branch, Rathgael House, Balloo Road, Bangor, Co Down BT19 2PR Tel: 0247 270077.

The Education Grants Advisory Service (EGAS), part of the Family Welfare Association, provides information on money for students. A copy of their guide *Money to Study* is available from EGAS, c/o Family Welfare Association, 501-505 Kingsland Road, Dalston, London E8 4AU Tel: 071 254 6251.

Loans

You will also, whether you get a grant or not, be able to take out a student loan in the first year. Loans were introduced in 1990 as a means of sharing support between students, taxpayers and parents. You are free to decide whether you take out a loan and how much you wish to borrow – up to the maximum amount specified each year. The 1991/92 maximum loan facility is to £580 (£660 in London) and will be increased yearly. This loan has to start being repaid when your salary reaches 85% of the national average wage.

Contact the Student Loan Company Ltd, 100 Bothwell Street, Glasgow G2 7GD Tel: 0345 300900.

Sponsorship
Some companies are prepared to help financially, but sponsored students are usually expected to work for their sponsor at least during the long vacations.

There are also 'sandwich courses', where periods of work in industry or abroad alternate with periods of full-time study, eg business studies, science, technology and language courses.

It is estimated that over 5,800 students are being sponsored each year, two-thirds of whom are on engineering and technology courses. Two out of every three sponsored students are recruited by their sponsoring employer. See the booklist on page 67 for details of a useful publication.

Living at home
If you can, and want to, living at home, is generally cheaper. A means-tested grant of up to £1795 (1990/91) is available. Think carefully about this because much can be learnt during higher education about living and learning away from home.

Community Charge
At present, students pay Community Charge (or 'Poll Tax') at 20% of the rate in the area in which they study. If you have any questions about how much you will have to pay etc talk to the Student's Union at your place of study.

Disability allowances
For information and advice on allowances, personal care requirements etc that are available to young people with disabilities contact 'Skill', The National Bureau for Students with Disabilities, 336 Brixton Road, London SW9 7AA.

30
Job hunting

If you decide you wish to leave school, rather than proceeding to higher education, you will need to decide what type of work you feel would best suit you. Talk to your careers adviser, your County Council Careers Service and anyone you know who you feel can give you insight into different jobs.

You can register with your local Jobcentre and employment agencies. Your local Careers Office will have lots of information that you can browse through. They have free leaflets on different careers and are there to help you. You are not wasting their time. They also display vacancies that are on offer.

Look in local and national newspapers as they have advertisements for job vacancies. For example, Wednesday's *Independent* newspaper carries creative and media vacancies, Thursday's *Guardian* includes computing vacancies.

Remember that many people get jobs that have not been advertised. You can write to employers even if they have not advertised vacancies. Some employers keep a file of speculative letters and look through them when vacancies come up.

When applying for jobs it is now standard practice to send a CV (*Curriculum Vitae*) with a short, handwritten covering letter.

Your CV
A CV is a summary of your personal details such as name, address, home telephone number etc. It should also list your exam results, interests, any jobs you may have had and names of referees to approach for references. Try to restrict your CV to one side of A4 paper.

Tips

- ▲ include positions of responsibility held
- ▲ prepare a draft and ask someone to check it
- ▲ type the final version as neatly as possible
- ▲ make several copies of it
- ▲ if you use someone's name as a referee, always ask him or her first.

Letters of application

A letter accompanying your CV is of great importance to your application. It should be concise, stating clearly your motivation for applying for the particular job and why you think you are suitable for it. Do not be timid; it may be the only opportunity you have to sell yourself to the potential employer.

Tips

- ▲ apply for a job as soon as you hear about it
- ▲ use plain, unlined paper and black or blue ink
- ▲ check your spelling
- ▲ letters to 'Dear Sir', 'Dear Madam' or 'Dear Sirs' end 'Yours faithfully'; letters to a named person eg 'Dear Mrs Smith' end with 'Yours sincerely'.

Application forms

You may be required to fill in an application form. The following may help you:

- ▲ read through the whole form first before you start to write
- ▲ if you can, take a photocopy to practise on
- ▲ write clearly and neatly
- ▲ check your spelling
- ▲ answer all questions
- ▲ take a photocopy (if possible) before sending it off.

31
Interviews

'Ask someone to interview you so you can practise answering questions.'
Liz

Sometime in your second year you may be called for interviews either with higher education institutions, potential employers or providers of training. An interview is your opportunity to make a good impression and to sell yourself. However, do not be tempted to lie about any of your skills or past achievements. This will not benefit you in the long run as you will probably be found out, particularly if references are sought.

Try to find out as much as you can about what the company, college or university offers. You could find out such information by going to the local library, by ringing up the company itself and asking if they have any public information materials or by obtaining the relevant prospectus.

Some interview do's and dont's:

Do

- ▲ some research before the day
- ▲ find out where to go and who you are seeing
- ▲ arrive in plenty of time
- ▲ take a copy of what you wrote on the original form and any certificates etc
- ▲ have some questions of your own ready
- ▲ always expect to be asked *'Why you have applied to this particular institution or company?'*

- ▲ be positive about yourself and speak clearly
- ▲ think about your strengths and weaknesses
- ▲ dress smartly
- ▲ look at the interviewer when you are speaking and when he/she is speaking
- ▲ be honest, be yourself
- ▲ ask how long you will have to wait for a decision.

Don't

- ▲ be late
- ▲ start by asking how much the pay is (if at a job interview)
- ▲ answer all questions with one word answers
- ▲ be drawn into an argument or lose your temper
- ▲ be afraid to ask to have a question repeated or explained
- ▲ smoke or chew gum.

Remember that the important point about any interview is to use it as a valuable exercise to find out your strengths and weaknesses.

32
A year off?

Whether you are opting to go straight into employment or are planning to continue your formal education, you may be considering taking a year off. This is an important decision which will need to be taken in time for your applications for jobs or places in higher education. Take care to consider:

▲ Whether your selected employer or higher education institution will encourage or even accept deferred applications.

▲ How you would make the most of a year off.

▲ The potential benefits of employment followed by travel or vice versa.

▲ What you think that you would gain both personally and in terms of your selected courses of study.

▲ Just because taking a year off is popular does not make it compulsory nor necessarily even suitable for you.

▲ Do you want to take a year off now or after college, or both?

▲ What the various organisations can offer.

A *Year Off ... A Year On?* published by Hobsons Publishing Plc, Bateman Street, Cambridge CB2 1LZ Tel: 0223 354551, is a useful guide to the way in which a year off can be used constructively, at home and abroad.

Work experience

Some companies have 'gap year' schemes which provide work experience for pre-university students. If you are interested then contact the company's personnel department for more information. *Jobs in the 'Gap' Year*, published by ISCO, 12a – 18a Princess Way, Camberley, Surrey GU15 3SP Tel: 0276 21188, lists companies who offer office work to students during their year off.

The 'Year in Industry' (formerly Pre-Formation of Undergraduate Engineers or PFUE) has merged with IndEX and aims to find students industrial placements for a minimum of six months in between sixth form and higher education. Contact: The Year in Industry, Simon Building, University of Manchester, Oxford Road, Manchester M13 9PL Tel: 061 275 4395.

STEP provides placements for students between sixth form and higher education. Contact: Shell Technology Enterprise Programme (STEP), Shell (UK) Ltd, Shell Mex House, The Strand, London WC2R OXD.

Taking a job abroad can give you a great deal of experience, boost your confidence and enhance your CV. Look in your library for directories of overseas job opportunities or read *Working Holidays* available from the Central Bureau for Educational Visits and Exchanges, Seymour Mews, London W1H 9PE Tel: 071 486 5101 or 3 Bruntsfield Crescent, Edinburgh EH10 4HD Tel: 031 447 8024 or 16 Malone Road, Belfast BT9 5BN Tel: 0232 66418/9. *Working Holidays* gives information about 99,000 paid and voluntary work opportunities, and visa, insurance and medical requirements.

Publications are also available from: Vacation Work Ltd, 9 Park End Street, Oxford OX1 1JH Tel: 0865 241978.

GAP Activity Projects offer 18 to 19 year-olds who have taken A-levels a wide range of work experience during their 'gap' year. Contact: GAP Ltd, 7 King's Road, Reading, Berks RG1 3AA Tel: 0734 594914.

Volunteering

Volunteer work is usually available and can provide an extremely useful experience. Again, it will enhance your CV by showing that you have initiative.

Community Service Volunteers (CSV) find placements for anyone aged 16-35. You must be prepared to wait for at least four months. For more information contact: CSV, 237 Pentonville Road, London N1 9NJ Tel: 071 278 6601

You could also contact the International Volunteer Service (IVS) 188 Rounday Road, Leeds LS8 5PL Tel: 0532 406787, or IVS Northern Ireland at 122 Great Victoria Street, Belfast BT7 7BG Tel: 0232 238147.

Volunteer Work is a useful booklet listing organisations who recruit volunteers for projects in the UK and countries worldwide. Contact: The Central Bureau (see the address on page 58). If you are interested in conservation work contact the British Trust for Conservation Volunteers (BTCV), 36 St Mary's Street, Wallingford, Oxon OX10 0EU.

Also try local offices of major charities such as Oxfam. They might be able to offer you some work as a volunteer.

Operation Raleigh offers a wide variety of expeditions to 17- to 25-year-olds. You need to be in good health and able to swim 500 metres. Contact: Operation Raleigh, Alpha Place, Flood Street, London SW3 5SZ Tel: 071 351 7541.

VSO offer posts for a minimum of two years. You must be experienced, skilled and at least 20 years old. Contact: VSO, Enquiries Unit, 317 Putney Bridge Road, London SW15 2PN Tel: 081 780 2266.

Project Trust is an educational charity offering projects of about one year to young people aged between 17- and 19-years-old. The projects aim to give young people the opportunity of living and working in countries outside Europe, usually in the developing world. Contact: Project Trust, Breacachadh Castle, Isle of Coll, Argyll PA78 6TB Tel: 08793 444(5).

Project 67 Limited places volunteers aged 18 and over in kibbutzim and moshavim (communal agricultural settlements) on working holidays in Israel. Contact: Project 67 Limited, 10 Hatton Garden, London EC1N 8AH Tel: 071 831 7626.

Travelling

Travelling can be an exciting way of learning, enjoying friends company and meeting people. You will need to plan and budget your trip carefully.

▲ If you need to earn money while you travel, find out which countries you will be allowed to work in and how to obtain permission.

▲ Make sure you have the correct medical advice, injections etc for the countries you are visiting. Contact the appropriate embassy who should be able to point you in the right direction.

33
Exam results

Your results

You are strongly advised to finish your summer holidays by the date on which your exam results are to be published. You will need to be available to deal with your application personally and quickly, particularly if you need to enter Clearing.

If you achieve the results required for your chosen course of study or career – well done. If proceeding to higher education, make sure you have applied for finance (as soon as you get the forms) and sort out accommodation at your new place of study.

You may be lucky and have a place in a hall of residence. If not, contact the housing department who should have lists of private accommodation available. Failing that you may have to obtain copies of local newspapers and check out the 'Accommodation to Let' sections because there may be a lot of competition for housing. Start looking as soon as you can.

Clearing

> *'Don't wait for your Clearing forms to arrive – as soon as you know your results get on the phone and beg! Be persistent as it shows you are really interested.'*
>
> James

It may be that you will not achieve the grades you were hoping for. This is not the end of the world. Many students get into university, college or polytechnic by applying through Clearing.

Think carefully about which courses you would find acceptable and those that you do not wish to consider. You will have to be flexible (ie can you find courses similar to your preferred one?), perhaps modular courses that include your favourite subject combined with others or alternative institutions.

Having drawn up your lists of courses and telephone numbers, do not delay. If you meet the minimum points score then ring up your first-choice college and ask if they will consider you. It may take some time to get through to the admissions tutor for your course but keep trying – it is worth the effort.

Clearing continues for a number of weeks. Above all, don't give up. You can even ring departments at the beginning of term as people drop out at the last minute.

The Independent on Sunday and Wednesday's *Independent* carry lists of course vacancies every week from the end of August until October. This information is also available via the electronic databases ECCTIS 2000, Campus 2000 and Polytel (polytechnics only).

Appealing against grading

If you feel that one or more of your grades does not accurately reflect your performance in the examinations, it is possible to appeal. Ask your school or college for advice.

Any candidate may appeal. You can either have your paper remarked or you can have a report on the remark. You or your school will have to meet all the costs yourself, and this can become expensive.

34
Retakes

If you do not manage to get a place through Clearing, it's time to reconsider your future. You have two main options – either retake your exams or do something completely different!

Retakes need not be a humiliating step. You will probably find that other friends are in the same boat. You do not, however, have to return to the same school or college, or study the same topics within your subject (although it might be an advantage).

You should check first with admissions tutors at higher education establishments to see what their policy is regarding retake applicants. Some highly competitive courses offer no second chances; others will see your willingness to retake as proof of your commitment and may make the same or only slightly higher offers the second time around.

Motivation will be a key factor when considering retakes. You may find that by having a complete change of scene or by going to a private tutorial college you will be spurred on. However, if you do decide to opt for a private college check what their reputation is like.

The cost of improving your grades will vary from £100 to £200 in fees in a local authority college, to up to £12,000 per year for retaking three A-levels with a good private tutor. Cost will therefore be a major factor when deciding which route to take.

For a list of private tutorial colleges, contact the Conference for Independent Further Education Colleges, Buckhall Farm, Bull Lane, Bethersden, Nr Ashford, Kent Tel: 0233 820797.

Mature students

Remember that you do not necessarily have to have A-levels to get on to a degree course. Polytechnics, colleges and most universities now accept substantial numbers of 'mature' students (ie 21-plus) without formal entry qualifications. In three years, therefore, you could get straight in to a higher education establishment.

The following publications may be useful;

University Entrance: Mature students – universities welcome you available free from UCCA, PO Box 28, Cheltenham, Glos GL50 1SA.

Open Doors to Higher Education – Opportunities for Everyone Over 21 from the Committee of Directors of Polytechnics (CDP), Kirkman House 12-14 Whitfield Street, London W1P 6AX Tel: 071 637 9939.

The other option is to take an Open University (OU) degree. The OU offers degree level courses to adults on a 'first-come-first-served' basis. You do not need qualifications to be accepted. Information can be obtained from The Open University, PO Box 71, Walton Hall, Milton Keynes MK7 6AA Tel: 0908 274066.

The SWAP (Scottish Wider Access Programme) is directed at mature students in Scotland. Contact: SWAP c/o Stevenson College of Further Education, Bankshead Avenue, Edinburgh 11.

35
Self-employment

You may consider that you have a sound business idea which you would like to implement. You need to calculate whether or not your business idea is financially viable. Research the market carefully and be sure there is considerable scope for your idea.

Consider the pros and cons of investment and self-employment:

Pros

- ▲ you are responsible for your own work
- ▲ if the idea is good and the business successful then you will reap the rewards
- ▲ if you run a business successfully for a few years you will have a valuable asset to sell.

Cons

- ▲ if things go wrong, you are entirely responsible
- ▲ debts and liabilities will be your responsibility
- ▲ are you the right kind of person to be self-employed?

Being self-employed means taking on a great deal of responsibility and being prepared to take decisions. You may initially have to work long hours for little money. Above all you need enthusiasm and motivation.

It will suit some people and not others. Get advice from people you know and organisations with experience of small businesses.

The Prince's Youth Business Trust offers help to 18- to 25-year-olds wanting to start their own business. Contact: The Prince's Youth Business Trust, Fifth Floor, 5 Cleveland Place, London SW1Y 6JJ Tel: 071 321 6500.

Livewire provides a free advice network, personal advice and an action planning pack. Contact: Livewire, 60 Grainger Street, Newcastle upon Tyne, NE1 5JG Tel: 091 261 5584.

Instant Muscle is a charity which helps unemployed young people to set up their own business. Contact: Instant Muscle, 84 Northend Road, London W14 9EF Tel: 071 603 2604.

Addresses of Local Enterprise Agencies can be found in the Yellow Pages.

36 Useful books

The following is a list of useful books and addresses. Other sources have been noted throughout the book.

Making a choice at 16+; *Making a choice at 18+* published by Letts

School Leavers Handbook edited by Jacquie Hughes, published by Bloomsbury

A/AS-Levels; National Diplomas - What next? published by the DES (see address below) is a useful booklet which gives details of the higher education options that are available. It also includes a list of useful publications and places to contact for further information.

Also published by the DES are *Higher Education - finding your way* by David Dixon, HMSO and *Student grants and loans: a brief guide* available from the DES, Publications Despatch Centre, Honeypot Lane, Stanmore, Middlesex HA7 1AZ Answerphone: 081 952 2366.

UCCA Handbook and *PCAS Guide for Applicants* are available free of charge from UCCA and PCAS PO Box 67, Cheltenham, Glos GL50 3SF Tel: 0242 222444 (UCCA) and 0242 526225 (PCAS). From 1992 there is a joint application form.

Polytechnic Courses Handbook is available from the Committee of Directors of Polytechnics (CDP), Kirkman House, 12-14 Whitfield Street, London W1P 6AX Tel: 071 637 9939. CDP also produces a number of other publications about polytechnics – write and request a list of them.

University Entrance 1992: The Official Guide published annually on behalf of the Committee of Vice-Chancellors and Principals by Sheed and Ward, 2 Creechurch Lane, London EC3A 5AQ.

Which Degree? published by Newpoint. Summarises courses available by subject and covers all types of institution.

Sunday Times Good University Guide is a consumer's guide to higher education facilities.

Handbook for Initial Teacher Training, Other Degree and Advanced Courses published annually by National Association of Teachers in Further and Higher Education. Available from Linneys ESL Ltd, Newgate Lane, Mansfield, Notts, NG18 2PA Tel: 0623 656565.

Guide to the Colleges and Institutes of Higher Education Administration Officer, Edge Hill College, Ormskirk L39 4QP Free.

A Compendium of Advanced Courses in Colleges of Further and Higher Education published annually, lists a wide range of courses outside the universities and is particularly good for advanced art courses and non-degree higher education such as journalism. From London and South East Regional Advisory Council for Education and Training, 232 Vauxhall Bridge Road, London SW1V 1AU.

Survey of HND Courses by Eric Whittington published by Trotman.

Sponsorships published by Careers and Occupational Information Centre (COIC). COIC also produces information about work, lifeskills and job change. Contact them at COIC, Moorfoot, Sheffield S1 4PQ Tel: 0742 594568 or COIC Scotland, 5 Kirk Loan, Corstorphine, Edinburgh EH12 7HD Tel: 031 334 0353.

The following titles are available from Hobsons Publishing Plc, Bateman Street, Cambridge CB2 1LZ Tel: 0223 354551. Ask them to send you a copy of their careers publications catalogue.

Decisions at 15/16+; *Decisions at 17/18+*; *Your Choice of Degree and Diploma*; *A Year Off... A Year On?*; *Which Subject? Which Career?*; *Jobs and Careers after A-levels*; *Sandwich Courses*; *Part-time Degrees, Diplomas and Certificates 1990/91*; *Graduate Studies* and *The Directory of Further and Higher Education* published annually; *Degree Course Guides* – individual guides are available for each subject, and *The Job Book*.

The Independent Schools Careers Organisation (ISCO) publishes a number of useful reference books:

Jobs in the 'Gap' Year (published January 1992).

The 1992 Sixth former's guide to visiting universities, polytechnics and colleges (published January 1992) and *Directory of Independent Further Education Colleges.*

For full details contact them at ISCO, 12a-18a Princess Way, Camberley, Surrey GU15 3SP Tel: 0276 21188.

Appendix A: Syllabus and coursework chart

You may find it useful to record the following details for each of your subjects.

Subject _____

▲ Examining Body _____

▲ Syllabus Number _____

Method of Assessment

▲ Number of examinations _____ % of total _____

▲ Number of pieces of
coursework required _____ % of total _____

▲ Number of practical
assessments _____ % of total _____

Subject _____

▲ Examining Body _____

▲ Syllabus Number _____

Method of Assessment

▲ Number of examinations _____ % of total _____

▲ Number of pieces of
coursework required _____ % of total _____

▲ Number of practical
assessments _____ % of total _____

Subject _____

▲ Examining Body _____

▲ Syllabus Number _____

Method of Assessment

▲ Number of examinations _____ % of total _____

▲ Number of pieces of
coursework required _____ % of total _____

▲ Number of practical
assessments _____ % of total _____

Subject _____

▲ Examining Body _____

▲ Syllabus Number _____

Method of Assessment

▲ Number of examinations _____ % of total _____

▲ Number of pieces of
coursework required _____ % of total _____

▲ Number of practical
assessments _____ % of total _____

Appendix B: Two year planner

Year 1

| | Sept | Oct | Nov | Dec | Jan | Feb |

Examinations

Coursework

Field Trips

Year 2

| | Sept | Oct | Nov | Dec | Jan | Feb |

Examinations

Coursework

Field Trips

Mar   Apr   May   June   July   Aug

Mar   Apr   May   June   July   Aug

Appendix C: Weekly timetable

	Per week
Course lessons	_____ hours
Other lessons (eg tutorial time, general studies, sport)	_____ hours
Free periods	_____ hours
Total	_____ hours

For example, if your waking hours are from 8am-11pm (ie 15 hours per day), then by estimating how long you think you will spend on academic work, travelling, meals and part-time work you can work out how much time you have left for other activities:

15 hours x 7 days =	105
less academic work (ie approx 35 hours per week)	<u>35</u>
leaving	70
less meals, travelling time etc	<u>25</u>
leaving	45
less part-time work (say 10 hours per week)	<u>10</u>
leaving	35

35 hours are left for all you have to do, and want to do.

Do your own arithmetic to work out your own timetable. You may find that there are not enough hours in which to do everything. If some things have to be dropped, make a decision about what you really want to do. You may wish to construct your own weekly timetable.

Appendix D: Important dates to remember

First year

March/April   Start thinking about options open to you in higher education and employment; find out about visits and Open Days (these usually occur between March and July).

May/June   Start making more detailed investigations. Visit your local careers service and ask your teachers for advice.

June/July   Attend Open Days and obtain prospectuses. Try to start making preliminary decisions especially if you think you want to go to Oxford or Cambridge university.

Second year

September   Draft out your forms, particularly if applying to Oxford or Cambridge. For Oxford you must submit an Oxford application card to the Oxford Colleges Admissions Office by 15 October; for Cambridge the Preliminary Application Form must be submitted by 15 October.

October   Ensure rough and completed forms are handed in.

November   Interviews, offers and rejections. Check carefully on instructions provided on how to reply to offers.

December   Deadline for UCCA/PCAS is December 15. It is possible to apply later, but institutions consider late applications at their own discretion.

January   Register intention to apply for a grant with the LEA in whose area you will have a permanent address at 30 June in the year you start.

May   Make a decision on which offers to hold.

August   Do not be too far from home and sources of advice and help as the exam results come out mid-month. Chase up your offers. If you were unsuccessful start looking at other courses which may be open to you.

September   Clearing operations start. See Chapter 33 (page 61) for advice on Clearing. Some courses start.

October   Most courses start.